I0426046

USMC FINANCIAL GUIDEBOOK
FOR
COMMANDERS

Headquarters, U.S. Marine Corps
NAVMC 2664 REV 1.0
PCN 10001335200

DEPARTMENT OF THE NAVY
HEADQUARTERS UNITED STATES MARINE CORPS
3000 MARINE CORPS PENTAGON
WASHINGTON, DC 20350-3000

NAVMC 2664
RFR
APR 3 2009

FOREWORD

1. PURPOSE

The successful management of limited resources is a true measure of a Commander's ability to effectively prioritize and employ forces to defeat the enemy. Sound financial management facilitates the Marine Corps mission – *to make Marines and Win Battles*. This guidebook is intended to be a ready reference desk guide that the USMC Commander can use to identify fiscal requirements, allocate financial resources, execute a budget, prepare for audits and inspections, and comply with Federal law, as well as Navy and Marine Corps policies. The information contained in this document was checked for accuracy at the time of editing. However, the information may be outdated due to the dynamic nature of financial management, and the frequently changing policy environment. Therefore, this guidebook should be used as an informational guide, and before any action is taken, it is recommended that the reader check with the command Comptroller for the most up-to-date policies.

2. CANCELLATION

NAVMC 2664 of June 12, 1998.

3. INFORMATION

Your command and legal responsibilities make you accountable and responsible for your activity's financial management team. Accordingly, Commanders need to be aware of their responsibilities as a fund manager as detailed in the Department of Defense Financial Management Regulation (DoD FMR), Volume 14, Chapter 1. To assist you, this publication provides a description of your basic financial management responsibilities and procedures.

4. REQUISITIONS

For requisitioning instructions, refer to MCO P5600.31G W/CH 1-3, Marine Corps Publications and Printing Regulations.

5. CERTIFICATION

Reviewed and approved this date.

D. D. Thiessen, Lieutenant General
Deputy Commandant, Programs and Resources

DISTRIBUTION STATEMENT A: Approved for public release; distribution is unlimited.

DISTRIBUTION: PCN 10001335200

LOCATOR SHEET

Subj: USMC FINANCIAL GUIDEBOOK FOR COMMANDERS

Location: _____

(Indicate location(s) of copy (ies) of this Manual.)

RECORD OF CHANGES

Please log completed change action as indicated.

Change Number	Date of Change	Date Entered	Signature of Person Incorporated Change

CONTENTS

CHAPTER I

USMC BUDGET

INTRODUCTION

Financial Management is inherent in command. Your job is to ensure funds entrusted to you are legally and judiciously spent.

Since the onset of Operation Iraqi Freedom, annual Emergency Supplemental spending bills to finance the costs of operations in Iraq and Afghanistan, as well as training, pre- and post-deployment, and equipment reset/reconstitution costs have provided a significant increase to the Marine Corps Total Obligation Authority (TOA). However, with Supplemental costs expected to migrate to the Marine Corps baseline in Fiscal Year (FY) 2010 and competing federal spending priorities putting pressure on future year Department of Defense (DoD) budgets, Commanders must ensure they are able to effectively articulate requirements and place constrained resources where they will best accomplish unit missions and objectives.

OVERVIEW OF THE PPBE PROCESS

The Planning Programming Budgeting and Execution (PPBE) Process serves as the means for allocating resources and is a continuous overlapping cycle. Deputy Commandant, Programs and Resources (DC P&R), in concert with the other Deputy Commandants (DC), formulates the Marine Corps planning guidance which in turn supports the planning guidance directed by the President of the United States (POTUS), Joint Chiefs of Staff (JCS), and the Secretary of Defense (SECDEF). The Commandant's Planning Guidance (CPG) and the Marine Corps Master Plan (MCMP) serve as the base documents for building your program and your budget. For Battalion level commands, your supply officer will work in concert with the Comptroller on the various budget calls. These documents can be provided to you by your servicing Comptroller. As a Commander, the following major PPBE cycles impact you.

The Program Objective Memorandum (POM) operates as a means for the Marine Corps to "right-size" requirements and programs. It translates into a 6 year Defense Program. The POM occurs during even years. For example, POM 12 will be conducted in FY 2010. During odd years, a program review will occur. This review allows Commanders to tweak the work accomplished during the POM. As a Commander, your role in the POM process is relatively straightforward; every two years articulate what you can do within constraints of POM funding, or ceiling tracks, and what you can't do with the funding you don't get. Requirements should be prioritized as Mission Critical, Mission Essential, or Mission Enhancement, and include urgent emerging requirements. POM submissions and request for funds should include tangible, defensible metrics, not generalities or unsubstantiated dire predictions.

Do not use the POM as a time to identify one time requirements; rather use it as a time to identify programmatic changes. A Base Operations Support increase due to migration of Navy F-18 squadrons, Reserve Squadrons, and other service squadrons to Cherry Point in the future provides an example of a programmatic increase that will require future year funding. Loss of the Riverine Operations mission provides an example of a programmatic decrease in future years. A requirement for $1K to replenish lost SL3 components or $150K to install an elevator in a building do not constitute POM initiatives; rather, they are simply current year budget shortfalls which should be addressed during year of execution either through the existing budget or through a mid year review. **It is a Commander's responsibility to identify programmatic changes that both increase and decrease funding requirements.**

The Deputy Commandants and the heads of the special staff agencies oversee the POM process within their sponsorship areas. The Programs and Resources (P&R) Department is the principal staff agency responsible for developing and defending the Marine Corps financial requirements, policies, and programs. The DC P&R owns the Marine Corps resource allocation process and serves as the principal adviser to the Commandant on all financial matters.

P&R provides budgetary guidance and appropriation ceilings to the MARFOR level commands. The MARFORs then provide their subordinate Commanders with this guidance coupled with MARFOR specific guidance. Commanders should coordinate with their next higher level when preparing their POM submission.

Budget Formulation serves to provide Commanders with a tool to prioritize their requirements and identify deficiencies to higher headquarters. The budget has its roots in the POM development. At the HQMC level, the budget submitted to the President is a 2 year plan; however, for all commands below the CMC level, the budget numbers should be provided by your Comptroller after each budget cycle (in June for the NAVCOMPT budget, in October for the OSD budget, and in January for the President's budget). Typically, the budget you receive in June reflects planning documents spreading your budget among your subordinate commands. This June budget also serves as an opportunity to identify shortfalls. You need to provide details and justification and then prioritize these shortfalls based on the guidance provided to you by your Comptroller. Budget Adjustments will be made once the appropriation bill is signed into law. Various changes will be assessed that might impact the numbers you previously received.

In order for HQMC to answer budget questions, Commander's need to articulate what the budget buys. Many of the Congressional cuts the Marine Corps receives are because of an inability to explain why we spent the money the way we did. The ability to articulate why we spend our money on a requirement that is coded for both Global War on Terror (GWOT) use and Garrison use, such as contracted support, serves as a good example. **HQMC cannot articulate the "whys" to Congress without the assistance of Commanders.**

Mid Year Review typically starts in the Spring and offers a Commander an opportunity to reassess their requirements during year of execution. At this time, Commanders should reassess priorities and submit any shortfalls up the chain of command.

Budget Execution is continuous. Most Commanders will receive the preponderance of their funds from the Operation and Maintenance appropriation – a one year appropriation. During the year of execution, a Commander will execute his budget based on the plan he prepared. The critical aspects of this job will comprise the remainder of this manual.

MONEY FLOW

The funds distribution process reflected within the accounting system begins with HQMC (P&R) issuing operating budgets or allotments to Commanders. Funding flows down the chain of command to the operating forces. Legal responsibility is passed down the chain of command with the flow of funds. This is referred to as "1517 responsibility." Title 31 United State Code

Section 1517 (31 U.S.C. 1517) makes obligating or expending in excess of the apportionment or reapportionment a crime. **Commanders are ultimately responsible for funds as they move down the chain of command**

In the absence of an annual Defense spending bill appropriated by Congress and signed into law by the president, the Marine Corps may start the fiscal year under a Continuing Resolution Authority (CRA). A CRA allows Commanders the latitude to continue normal operations and maintenance until a Defense spending bill is passed; however, no new initiatives or "new starts" may be executed. An example of a new start would be a large contract that had not previously been in place.

The funds flow hierarchy is as follows:

- HQMC. HQMC issues operating budgets (OPBUD's) and allotments which provide funding authority from a specific appropriation to a command to accomplish its mission. OPBUD/allotment authority is expressed in terms of a specific amount granted to incur obligations and payments in support of assigned missions and functions.

   o OPBUD/ Sub-Operating Budget (SUBOPBUD). An OPBUD is the annual budget of an activity (responsibility center) stated in terms of functional/sub-functional categories and cost accounts. It contains estimates of the total value of all resources required for mission performance of an activity, including reimbursable work and/or services for others. OPBUDs are issued by HQMC to all responsibility centers. SUBOPBUDs are issued by designated responsibility centers to certain subordinate commands.

   o Allotments. The authority, expressed in terms of a specific amount of funds granted to a Commander by the Commandant, to obligate and expend funds for a particular purpose. Obligation and expenditure of the funds may not exceed the amount specified in the allotment, and a command must adhere to the purpose for which the authorization is made.

- Major Command Recipient Identifier (MRI). A Major Command Recipient is a command that receives funds directly from HQMC. Major Command Recipients may pass funds to Allotment Recipients within their command. Commander, U.S. Marine Corps Forces Pacific; Commander, U.S. Marine Corps Forces Command; Commander, Marine Corps Logistics Command; and Commander, Marine Corps Combat Development Command are examples of Major Command Recipients.

- Allotment Recipient Identifier (ARI). An ARI is a command that receives an allotment or OPBUD from a MRI. Commander, Marine Corps Installations East and Commander, Marine Corps Installations West are examples of ARIs. MRIs are also ARIs when they pass funds to themselves. An example of a MRI that passes funds to themselves as an ARI is Commander, Marine Corps Forces Pacific.

- Suballotment Recipient Identifier (SRI). A SRI is a subordinate command that receives a portion of an allotment or OPBUD from an ARI. Examples of SRIs are Marine Corps Air Station Miramar, Marine Corps Base Camp Pendleton, and I Marine Expeditionary Force (MEF). Major Command Recipients are also

Allotment/Suballotment Recipients when they pass funds to themselves. SRI is the lowest level at which legal responsibility (31 U.S.C. 1517 authority) can be passed.

- Work Center Identifier (WCI). A Work Center is a subdivision of a SRI. These activities are held administratively responsible.

- Budget Execution Activity (BEA). A BEA is a subdivision of a Work Center. Legal responsibility for the proper management of the funds is retained by the SRI or WCI holder. An example of a BEA is the facilities department within a base or a battalion within the MLG, DIV, or MAW.

- Budget Execution Sub-Activity (BESA). A BESA is a subdivision of a BEA. A BESA is established to capture detailed costs below the BEA and are the lowest organizational level to which funding is broken down in the Marine Corps. BESAs for all O&MMC funded activities have been standardized and are listed by applicable WCI in the standalone Financial Code Manual referenced in Appendix B.

TYPES OF APPROPRIATION

Appropriations exist to exert control over government costs. Different appropriations exist in order to finance differing types of requirements. Using one appropriation to finance requirements properly financed in another appropriation is a violation of the "Purpose Statute" and could lead to a violation of the "Antideficiency Act"

The Marine Corps receives six appropriations. Four are annual appropriations (Military Personnel Active and Reserve, and Operations and Maintenance Active and Reserve), and two are multi-year procurement appropriations (Procurement, Marine Corps and Procurement Ammunition, Navy and Marine Corps). The Marine Corps has access to Nonappropriated fund sources and Navy Working Capital funds. The Marine Corps also uses funds appropriated to the Navy and DoD.

An overview of major appropriations is below:

Marine Appropriations sometimes referred to as **Green Appropriations** are controlled directly by the Marine Corps. This funding is used to pay Marines, procure equipment, pay for training, buy food, fuel and spare parts, maintain military buildings, pay civilian salaries, and support quality of life requirements such as community services.

- Military Personnel, Marine Corps (MPMC) – This annual appropriation impacts all Active Duty Marines. It provides for military pay, allowances, clothing, subsistence, and permanent change of station moves. This is the largest appropriation received by the Marine Corps and is HQMC centrally administered by HQMC. (Note: the Marine Corps Junior ROTC program is funded with O&MMC, and associated clothing is funded with MPMC.)

- Reserve Personnel, Marine Corps (RPMC) – This annual appropriation provides for pay, allowances, clothing, per diem, travel, and other related costs for Reserve Marine Corps Personnel, including Reserve officer candidates, and Reserve officers assigned to active duty under 10 U.S.C. 265. HQMC centrally administers some of this appropriation but provides select commands with the ability to execute transactions in support of annual training duty travel and per diem, and that portion dealing with clothing which, for control purposes, is given out in specific amounts to designated responsibility centers.

- Operations and Maintenance, Marine Corps (O&MMC) – This annual appropriation provides the funds to finance the costs of Marine Corps operations and maintenance. This appropriation serves as the primary source of funds to operating forces and installation commanders. Commanders use these funds to purchase supplies from the Navy Working Capital Fund, utilities, civilian labor, open market purchases, and temporary additional duty, just to name a few. O&MMC is also a source of Marine Corps Community Services (MCCS) appropriated funds. This appropriated fund (APF) support is provided via the Uniform Funding and Management (UFM) procedures for morale, welfare and recreation (MWR) programs (discussed in the Nonappropriated Fund (NAF) section). MCCS also relies on NAF and OSD financial support for key DoD-wide family and Marine support programs.

- Operation and Maintenance, Marine Corps Reserve (O&MMCR) – This annual appropriation supports the day-to-day operation of Reserve programs.

- Procurement, Marine Corps (PMC) – This three-year appropriation finances the purchase of weapons, tracked combat vehicles, guided missiles and equipment, communications and electronic equipment, support vehicles, engineer and other support equipment, spares and repair parts.

- Procurement of Ammunition, Navy and Marine Corps (PANMC) – This three-year appropriation finances the purchase of ammunition and related items.

Navy Appropriations sometimes referred to as **Blue Appropriations** represent the direct support portions of the Navy's budget spent on the Marine Corps that are in addition to Marine Corps "green dollar" appropriations. Blue dollars pay to procure, operate and maintain Marine Corps aircraft, provide Navy Corpsman and Chaplains, and other direct support items not covered by green appropriations. These specific "Blue" dollar support efforts for the Marine Corps are often called "Blue in Support of Green" (BISOG). Other Navy support to the Marine Corps includes the cost of Navy personnel serving in Marine Corps organizations (Military Personnel, Navy); aircraft purchased for the Marine Corps inventory (Aircraft Procurement, Navy); aircraft fuel and maintenance, specifically authorized aviation-related materials and supplies (O&M, Navy); equipment purchased by Marine Aviation units (Other Procurement, Navy); development costs for Marine Corps equipment and other programs (Research, Development, Test and Evaluation, Navy (RDT&E,N)); and Marine Corps requirements for new military construction projects (Military Construction, Navy (MILCON), Military Construction, Naval Reserves (MCNR), and Family Housing, Navy and Marine Corps (FHN&MC)). There are many other areas of Navy support which are less visible, such as that portion of the cost of the Navy's air training command that goes to support the Marine Corps, and the funding of various civilian training programs.

Navy Working Capital Fund (NWCF) acts as a self-sufficient operation with funds generated through the sale of goods and services to customers to replenish the costs of goods and services sold. Costs of goods and services to customers incorporate all administrative, overhead, labor, and materials costs and these charges are passed with a small surcharge to the customer. The funds received by the NWCF from the operating forces for goods and services sold become the source of funds used to finance future operations. Supply operations of NWCF provide for standard items of material, subsistence, petroleum, oil, lubricants, maintenance parts and assemblies, and minor items of equipment of a consumable nature where there is a recurring demand. NWCF funds are not annually appropriated, but work off a revolving fund concept. An example of a NWCF funded activity is the Depot Maintenance Activity (DMA) at Albany, GA.

Nonappropriated Funds (NAF) are government funds other than those appropriated by the Congress. The funds are generated by NAF Instrumentalities (NAFIs) authorized by competent authority for the morale, welfare, comfort and/or recreation of military personnel or civilian employees. Command level NAF retail, food/hospitality, billeting, and recreation outlets generate proceeds from operations used to supplement appropriated funds in providing MWR programs and facilities. All Marine Corps NAF activities are instrumentalities of the U.S. Government and as such are entitled to all the immunities and privileges available to governmental agencies. Despite the fact that these funds are generated by internal Marine Corps activities and not appropriated by Congress, they are government funds, and are subject to strict legal rules. Since NAF activities are an integral part of base and station operations, they merit appropriated fund support based upon the level authorized for each category of NAFI. APF support is provided to a NAF activity via a Memorandum of Agreement (MOA) in accordance with the Uniform Funding and Management (UFM) guidance provided by the Assistant Secretary of the Navy (Financial Management and Comptroller) (ASN (FM&C)) memo of 12 October 2004 and DoD Instruction 1015.15.

As a Commander, you will receive NAF funds from your MCCS representative to support morale and welfare functions for the Marines under your charge. These funds are referred to as Unit and Family Readiness Funds (U&FRF). U&FRF (incorporating the former picnic and party funds) are intended to support unit MWR needs including recreational, social, and family readiness activities. In an effort to make U&FRF simple and easy to use for Commanders, MCCS has taken action to establish a single NAF allocation per Marine per year, for units home-based at Marine Corps installations. This also applies to sailors or other service members assigned to the unit and in support of Marines. The funds are to be used in the year provided rather than accumulated over time. These funds shall not be carried over at NAF fiscal year-end (31 January). Funds will be allocated quarterly based on the onboard unit end strength for the command, as reported in Marine Corps Total Force System (MCTFS). More information about NAF funds can be obtained from MCO P1700.27B and your MCCS representative.

CHAPTER II

COMMAND FINANCIAL MANAGEMENT

OVERVIEW

The majority of funds allocated to the Marine Corps in the federal budget are committed to pay for 'fixed costs' and are not available for reprogramming to meet emergent or discretionary requirements. The Marine Corps manpower appropriation, for example, comprises 56.8% of the total USMC budget and is "fenced" to "buy" Marines. The actual discretionary funds that are available to each USMC Commander are therefore quite limited.

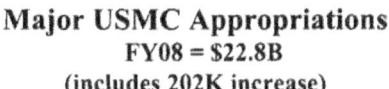

Major USMC Appropriations
FY08 = $22.8B
(includes 202K increase)

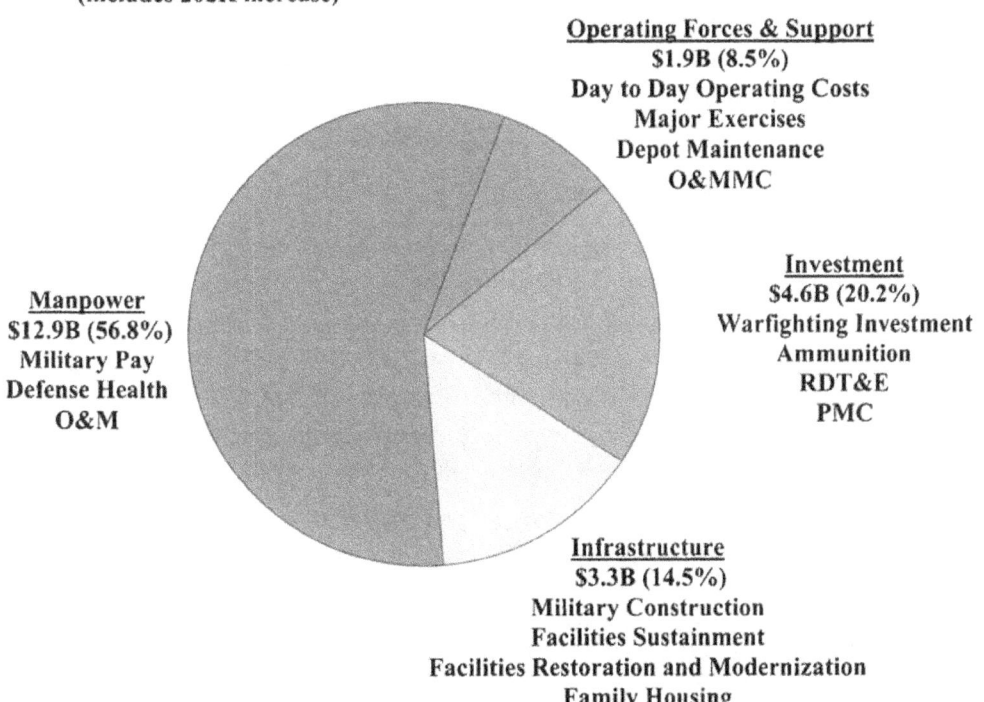

Operating Forces & Support
$1.9B (8.5%)
Day to Day Operating Costs
Major Exercises
Depot Maintenance
O&MMC

Investment
$4.6B (20.2%)
Warfighting Investment
Ammunition
RDT&E
PMC

Manpower
$12.9B (56.8%)
Military Pay
Defense Health
O&M

Infrastructure
$3.3B (14.5%)
Military Construction
Facilities Sustainment
Facilities Restoration and Modernization
Family Housing

COMMANDER'S FINANCIAL RESPONSIBILITY

The Antideficiency Act (ADA) consists of a series of federal statutes that make it illegal for government officials to spend money other than as Congress intends. If violated, the ADA requires a formal investigation process with the results reported to Congress. Violations can lead to adverse personnel actions and even criminal proceedings. There are three primary legal considerations affecting the Commander's responsibility with funds entrusted to him. The first is the "*Purpose* Statute" (31 U.S.C. 1301); the second legal consideration deals with the *time* money is available to spend (31 U.S.C. 1502); and the third legal consideration deals with *amounts* available to spend (31 U.S.C. 1517).

Purpose – An all-too-common pitfall for Commanders centers on violating the "Color of Money" or the "Purpose Statute," 31 U.S.C. 1341. This represents a legal violation and is required to be reported to the President via the Office of Management and Budget (OMB), Congress, and the Government Accountability Office (GAO). Disciplinary action taken must be spelled out in the letter. Congress appropriates funds to the Marine Corps for specific purposes, with the expectation that those funds will only be used for those purposes. Exceeding the minor construction threshold or using O&M to purchase centrally managed equipment (such as vehicles) that should have been purchased by Marine Corps Systems Command (MCSC) with PMC represent the most common Purpose Statute violations committed by Marine Corps Commanders.

The necessary expense doctrine falls under the purpose statute. It states that agencies may only spend appropriated funds for a necessary expense of the programs it is operating. In other words, appropriations, "shall be applied only to the objects for which the appropriations were made except as otherwise provided by law." The Comptroller General has issued many opinions indicating that expenditures for personal items, such as $400 watches or engraved K-bars, generally do not qualify as a necessary expense. Low cost items classified as personal gifts are not necessary expenses and may not be purchased with appropriated funds unless there is specific statutory authority to do so. Commanders are advised to coordinate with both their Comptroller and their local Area Counsel Office when questions arise. A three part necessary expense analysis applies:

- First, verify the expenditure is 'necessary' to accomplish the object of an appropriation, or will contribute materially to the accomplishment of that objective.
- Second, assess that the expenditure is *not prohibited by law*. This is done by reviewing the legislation for prohibitive language and restrictions.
- Third, determine if the expenditure is otherwise provided for. If there are two or more appropriations available for the expenditure, use the most specific appropriation.

Time – Congress grants funding for specific time periods and funds must be obligated during that period. Not only must money be obligated during its period of availability, but obligations must be a "Bona Fide Need" of that period. This rule mandates that money only be obligated to meet a legitimate or bona fide need arising in the fiscal year for which the appropriation was made. It restricts this year's appropriated funds from being used to fund next fiscal year's requirements. Purchasing items with annual funds appropriated for FY 2009 that will be stock piled and used in FYs 2010, 2011, and 2012 is a violation of the intent of Congress and is an ADA violation. Contracts may legally be entered into during one fiscal year and cross over into the next fiscal year. Examples include severable and non-severable contracts.

Severable contracts can be separated into components that independently meet a separate need of the government. Examples of severable service contracts include admin support, housekeeping services, and trash collection. Statutory authority exists that allows service contracts (and leases) to cross fiscal years. This is so an agency can space out their contracts and not have to start all contracts in October. These contracts can not exceed 12 months in duration.

Non-severable contracts produce a single outcome, product, or report that cannot be subdivided for separate performance. Examples include: overhaul of a ship, development of a software program, or an effort that will result in a end product. Training tends to be non-severable. In non-severable service contracts, the government must fund the entire effort with dollars available for obligation at the time the contract is executed. The contract performance may cross fiscal years and the period of performance may exceed 12 months.

Amount – Amount represents the final fiscal law principle. The bottom line is that you are not allowed to spend more than allotted to your command. This can be avoided by matching your annual budget to requirements, identifying and forwarding deficiencies for review and any additional funds that may become available, and periodically matching what funds you have remaining with the requirements you have pending. Rely on your Comptroller and remember early identification of a fiscal shortfall will increase likelihood of that shortfall being funded. **Violating a provision of the ADA means you broke the law.** This law cannot be ignored, waived, interpreted, or reengineered away. "I did it for the good of the Corps" is not an acceptable justification for breaking the law.

Obtain frequent financial status reports from your Comptroller/fiscal officer. These reports will show what is obligated compared to your authority. Just as importantly, they can show you what is committed that may or may not become an obligation. If you have commitments that are not obligated and exceed your authority, you will commit an ADA unless you cancel them or request and obtain additional funds from higher headquarters prior to incurring the obligation.

There may be a problem if, in any quarterly or annual period:

- Debit (negative) balances exist in a funding document received from another command
- Commitments exceed Obligations in an account
- Commitments exceed Authorizations in an account
- Obligations exceed Authorizations in an account
- Obligations fail to get properly recorded

REMEMBER: Violations of the Antideficiency Act must be reported by the Marine Corps Director, Fiscal Division via the ASN(FM&C), the Undersecretary of Defense (Comptroller), OMB, Congress, GAO, and Congress to the President. The report must include disciplinary action taken, as well as the names of responsible individuals.

EXPENSE/INVESTMENT CRITERIA

The basic rules for determining the "proper" appropriation to finance equipment purchases are found in the "expense/investment criteria." The following are the basic provisions:

- Equipment items that are "centrally managed" are investment items, regardless of cost.

- Non-centrally managed equipment items with a 'system unit cost' equal to or greater than the expense/investment threshold (currently $250,000) are investment items.

- Items of equipment that are not centrally managed and have a system unit cost of less than the expense/investment threshold are expense items.

References: 10 U.S.C. 2245a; DoDFMR Vol. 2A, Chap. 1; NAVSO P-1000, para. 075001

SYSTEM UNIT COST

The system unit cost is applied to the cost of a complete system rather than the cost of individual items of equipment or components that, when aggregated, become a system. The concept of a system must be considered in evaluating the procurement of an individual end item. A system is comprised of a number of components that are part of and function within the context of a whole to satisfy a documented requirement. The system unit cost is applied to the aggregate cost of all components being acquired as a new system, as additions or replacements to an existing system, or as stand-alone items. A validated requirement may not be fragmented or acquired in a piecemeal fashion in order to circumvent the expense/investment criteria. This is important to know because if you purchase pieces of a system separately, you will be committing an ADA violation by not adhering to the Purpose Statute.

CENTRAL MANAGEMENT

Central item management is defined as the management in the central supply system or a DoD-wide or Service-wide acquisition and control system in which the manager has the authority for management and procurement of items of equipment. In the Marine Corps, centrally managed items are purchased with the Procurement, Marine Corps (PMC) appropriation. MCSC is responsible for budgeting and executing all PMC. Therefore, if you have a requirement that happens to be a centrally managed item, you must contact MCSC to identify your need and make arrangements for them to purchase your requirement with PMC.

A reason assets are centrally managed is that there is a single entity to ensure the standardization of gear or equipment, a prioritized fielding plan, and an O&M sustainment funding tail. This is important for you to know because if you use your O&M to purchase something that is centrally managed, you will commit both a Purpose Statute violation and an ADA violation.

CENTRAL PROCUREMENT

A distinction must be made for items that are centrally managed versus centrally procured. Items are centrally procured if they are designated for initial procurement via a central agency. The prime example of a centrally procured item is the initial issue program for individual items of clothing and equipment managed by MCSC. Central procurement items may be either expense or investment items. If the items are expense items, replacement of items to achieve desired stockage levels are the responsibility of the using unit and funded with their O&MMC. Every centrally managed program is centrally procured; however, there are centrally procured programs that are not centrally managed, and are therefore expense items. NOTE: Another point of confusion is that often O&M funded *centrally procured* programs are called centrally managed programs (CMPs).

COMMAND BUDGET PLANNING

CMC provides budget guidance in MCO P7100.8, annual bulletins, and MARADMINs with specific guidance, including financial ceiling levels, for individual years. Comptrollers act as the Commander's fiscal representative. Comptrollers, with flag staff support, assist the Commanding General and his subordinate commanders in determining requirements and allocating resources. Comptrollers provide advice to Commanders on command fiscal status, and promote efficient resources utilization. Comptrollers are the staff officers responsible for formulating and promulgating budget guidance to command staff and subordinate commanders.

Commands without comptrollers are responsible for developing and executing a financial plan. Just like a family with a check book, Commanders must identify their fixed operating costs and develop a spending plan which meets fixed cost requirements. A Commander needs to know what types of funds his command will be allocated, what the limitations are on using those funds, and how the command may allocate or, if necessary, realign funds to meet requirements.

Essentially, there are four basic tasks involved in formulating the budget:

1. Identify operational requirements to meet command goals and the directives from higher authority. Requirements must be identified in a monthly Obligation Phasing Plan, which serves as a tracking mechanism to ensure proper execution.

2. Determine the cost involved in meeting the identified requirements.

3. Prioritize and justify requirements within the ceiling using the formats provided by higher headquarters. Clearly demonstrate your budget represents efficient and effective use of resources. Appropriate statistics should be included to reflect output to be achieved as a result of funding at the indicated level. Prioritization of the funding line and requirements that will not be executed facilitates unit deficiency identification and determination of mission impacts in the event you do not receive additional funding.

4. Identify and prioritize unfunded deficiencies. This list will be added to a HQMC database and used to identify priorities as funds become available. Explaining your shortfalls and identifying impacts to your command allows your higher headquarters, and HQMC, to ensure funds become available to pressing requirements. Before submitting a shortfall up the chain of command, you should look within your existing authority.

The command budget should be prepared with the same care applied to building a unit operation plan. The Commander's staff and subordinate unit commanders must be involved to ensure this plan truly supports operational requirements projected for the upcoming fiscal year.

Once a financial plan has been developed and begins to execute, the Commander needs to maintain awareness through periodic Status of Funds reports review. Your Comptroller or fiscal officer has access to these reports and should be briefing you on your status of funds weekly.

COMMAND BUDGET EXECUTION

There are ethical, legal, and policy issues each Commander should be familiar with concerning budget execution. Commanders need to understand the limitations and the flexibilities available for the types of funding over which they may have control. Commanders do not have complete discretion to spend money however they want. As described above, different 'types' of funding are intended for specific purposes, which means Commanders are legally limited in their funding flexibility. Commanders must work with their Comptroller or financial officer, and realize as frustrating as it may seem, that financial management is controlled by legal and ethical limitations.

CHAPTER III

MARINE CORPS MANAGERS' INTERNAL CONTROL PROGRAM (MCMIC)

INTRODUCTION

Commanders are responsible for implementing and monitoring an Internal Control Program (ICP). Internal controls continue to receive increased emphasis and are the focus of external audits. Internal controls apply to financial management as well as any area involving safety and operations within the Marine Corps. The Comptroller plays a role in coordinating audits for non-financial matters and serves as the primary lead for financial audits.

Congressional statutes, as implemented by OMB Circular A-123, provide guidance for implementing an ICP. A-123 concludes that the Commander ultimately remains responsible for developing and maintaining internal controls. Examples of internal controls are:

- Standard Operating Procedures
- Safety Rules
- Security Regulations
- Measurement Activities for Process Improvement, and
- Procurement and Fiscal Rules/Regulations

Commanders use the MCMIC Program to prevent or detect unauthorized acquisition, use or disposition of any command assets, and prevent waste, fraud, and abuse. Commanders' responsibilities for internal control under MCO 5200.24D include the development of effective management internal controls, the evaluation and correction of deficiencies, the use of effective follow-up procedures, and certain reporting requirements. Key elements of the MCMIC Program include:

- Programs, operations, functions, and processes achieve their intended results.
- People, equipment, and money use remain consistent with USMC and DON mission.
- Programs and resources remain protected from waste, fraud, and mismanagement.
- Laws and regulations are being followed.
- Revenues and expenditures are properly accounted for and recorded.
- Reliable and timely information has been obtained, maintained, reported and used for decision-making.

The MCMIC Program is comprised of two distinct processes, Internal Controls Over Financial Reporting (ICOFR) and Overall Managers' Internal Control (OMIC). Each process has the common purpose of providing reasonable assurance that effective and efficient internal controls are in place throughout the Marine Corps.

INTERNAL CONTROLS OVER FINANCIAL REPORTING (ICOFR) PROCESS

All Marine Corps Commands and HQMC Staff Agencies will cooperate fully with the staff of the Fiscal Division (Code RF) in identifying and documenting the most important internal controls supporting a targeted financial statement line item, and conducting operational tests of these controls to assure effectiveness. Responsible agencies will prepare, document, and track Corrective Actions Plans (CAPs) for resolving internal control weaknesses identified during the process.

OVERALL MANAGERS' INTERNAL CONTROL (OMIC) PROCESS

The OMIC Process requires all Marine Corps Commands (those reporting directly to the Commandant) and HQMC Staff Agencies to submit an annual report to the Commandant in the form of a Statement of Assurance (SOA) on the effectiveness of internal controls over all functions, programs, and operations under their authority.

Marine Corps Commanders will incorporate basic internal controls in their strategies, plans, guidance, and procedures governing their programs and operations. Managers should ensure that military and civilian personnel responsible for OMIC oversight are identified and that the respective fitness report or performance appraisal system reflects internal control responsibilities as required by SECNAVINST 5200.35E.

Internal controls are used daily by managers and employees to accomplish the identified organization objectives. Simply put, internal controls are the operational methods that enable work to proceed as expected. Most controls can be classified as preventive or detective.

Preventive controls discourage errors or irregularities. For example:

- Review of purchases prior to approval prevents inappropriate expenditures of command funds.
- A computer program, which asks for a password, prevents unauthorized access to information.

Detective controls identify an error or irregularity after it has occurred. Examples include:

- An exception report that detects and lists incorrect or incomplete transactions.
- A manager's review of long distance telephone charges that detects improper or personal calls that should not have been charged to the account.

The MCMIC Process:

- Identify Assessable Units
- Develop Managers' Internal Control (MIC) Plan
- Conduct Risk Assessments
- Evaluate Internal Controls
- Develop Corrective Action Plans
- Submit Required Certifications

In the Marine Corps, Internal Control Program responsibilities have been promulgated that detail the documentation and reporting requirements. The process includes identifying 'assessable units', which can be any organization, function, program or subdivision capable of being evaluated by an internal control procedure, and tied to a specific responsible manager. The list of assessable units within a command must include every command element.

MANAGERS' INTERNAL CONTROL (MIC) PLAN

The MIC Plan is a summary of a command's MIC program. The plan captures the organization's approach to implementing an effective internal control program. The MIC Plan should be updated as needed. The plan must identify the following key elements:

- The organization's MIC coordinator and the alternate MIC coordinator.
- An overview of the MIC program as it relates to GAO standards for internal controls.
- A description of risk assessment methodology.
- A description of monitoring/internal control assessment methodology.
- A description of how to develop and track corrective action plans.
- MIC training efforts.
- The date the plan was last updated.

RISK ASSESSMENTS

Risk Assessments require identifying analyzing, and managing internal and external risks that may affect achievement of an organizations mission or goals. It serves as a documented review by command leadership of an assessable unit's susceptibility to fraud, waste or abuse. Leadership evaluates the general control environment, analyzes the inherent risks, and arrives at a preliminary assessment of the safeguards for the assessable unit. It is a four step process:

- Describe the risk of the assessable unit
- Describe the established controls (or where they are documented)
- Describe test and results of test performed that ensures controls are working
- Describe corrective actions on identified weaknesses, estimated completion dates, and the person responsible for the correction.

INTERNAL CONTROL ASSESSMENT

Once internal controls are in place, leaders must actively monitor those controls to ensure they are functioning. Internal control assessments include both internal reviews and evaluations from external organizations such as audit organizations. Every assessable unit should conduct at least one internal control assessment annually. An internal control assessment does not need to include all controls each year. The scope of the internal control assessment is based on a leader's judgment. While documentation is required, there is no prescribed format for completing an internal control assessment for the OMIC Process. The goal is to maintain documentation that gives leaders the information they need to establish and improve internal controls.

CORRECTIVE ACTION PLANS (CAPS)

Corrective Action Plans are required for identified material weaknesses. Material weaknesses are specific instances of noncompliance of such importance as to warrant reporting to the next higher level of command.

MATERIAL WEAKNESS CRITERIA

The following list can be used to assist in deciding whether or not a control weakness is material:

- Impaired fulfillment of mission or operations
- Magnitude of funds, personnel, property, or other resources involved
- Frequency of actual or potential loss

- Current or probable Congressional or media interest (Note: any weaknesses in high visibility areas should be reported whether material or not; e.g., credit card purchases)
- Actual or potential loss of resources (e.g., personnel, inventory, property, etc.)
- Sensitivity of resources involved (e.g., drugs, munitions, etc.)
- Unreliable information causing unsound leadership decisions
- Violations of statutory or regulatory requirements
- Diminished credibility or reputation of management
- Deprivation of needed Government services to the public
- Impact on information security
- Leadership conflict of interest

MANAGERS' INTERNAL CONTROL PROGRAM STATEMENT OF ASSURANCE (SOA)

Each Command and each Headquarters Staff Agency must submit to the Commandant through Programs and Resources (P&R) Code RFR, an annual Statement of Assurance for the OMIC Process by the due date set by P&R (RFR). The SOA must be signed by the head (or Principal Deputy) of the component. The certification statement must include the elements prescribed in SECNAV M-5200.35.

The annual report will summarize internal control evaluation results and the command's rationale for the statements of reasonable assurance on internal controls effectiveness, including the number of evaluations performed and used by the command in the evaluation process. It must also include the number of evaluations planned for the following year.

AUDITS, INSPECTIONS, AND ASSIST VISITS

Although the term "audit" is often associated with the process of examining accounting records and related documents, the activities of audit agencies are seldom restricted to accounting matters. Audit scope is much broader and may extend into any aspect of an agency's operations. MCO 7510.3E applies to the audit function. It is important that Commanders know the purpose, scope, and authority of all organizations that oversee, audit, or inspect their commands. Audits of Marine Corps activities are conducted by several audit agencies.

The Naval Audit Service (NAS), GAO, and Department of Defense Inspector General (DoDIG) have statutory authority to review government management actions and publish audit reports consisting of findings, recommendations and management responses. Authority to audit Marine Corps NAFIs is delegated to the Commandant by the Secretary of the Navy (SECNAV).

NAS is headed by the Auditor General of the Navy, and performs all internal audits in the Department of the Navy (DON). All DON missions, functions, programs, and activities are subject to audits of mission performance, fiduciary responsibility, economy and efficiency, and financial transaction validity, as well as compliance with applicable laws and regulations.

During the conduct of audits within the Marine Corps, NAS auditors are authorized access to any management information consistent with the audit purpose, and auditor security clearance. NAS issues a letter with the audit objectives to the Commandant, Code RFR, who will then forward a copy of the letter to the appropriate offices at HQMC and field commands subject to the audit. NAS recommendations often relate to specific discrepancies and are addressed to the Commandant and specific field commands.

Commanders must pay special attention to audit reports that address the potential for "monetary benefits" or "funds put to better use". The decision by the Commander to concur, or non-concur in audits with such findings, must be carefully weighed to ensure the audit has reached conclusions based on valid, supportable evidence. Because of the potential impact of such findings, Commanders must reach an informed decision on concurring or nonconcurring with such findings.

GAO is an agency of Congress, conducts audits and reviews throughout the federal government. GAO representatives are external auditors to the Marine Corps, and are subject to more rigid guidelines under which they may obtain certain types of documents. GAO recommendations focus on system-wide weaknesses and are usually addressed to SECDEF / SECNAV. *SECNAVINST 5740.26B and MCO 7510.3E apply.*

DoDIG performs audits and reviews within DoD, similar to GAO. Requirements levied on DoDIG auditors for access to commands and information is the same as for GAO. Also, DoDIG recommendations usually address system-wide problems instead of command unique situations. *SECNAVINST 5740.25D and MCO 7510.3E apply.*

Surveys and Investigations Staff (S&IS) of the House Appropriations Committee (HAC) performs inquiries into Marine Corps issues as directed by the HAC, usually centering on current budget issues. S&IS reports are not provided to DoD for comment prior to delivery to the HAC. *SECNAVINST 5740.29A and MCO 5740.4B apply.*

Defense Contract Audit Agency (DCAA) is responsible for auditing all contracts with the DoD. *DoDD 5105.36 applies.*

MCNAFAS, under the operational and technical control of the Director, Fiscal Division, audits Marine Corps NAFIs. MCNAFAS is responsible for auditing Marine Corps nonappropriated fund activities including the Marine Corps exchanges, club systems, recreation funds, and miscellaneous NAFIs. *MCO 7510.2E applies.*

The Audit and Review Branch (RFR) within P&R coordinates and provides assistance with external audits and inspections to Marine Corps Commands and HQMC Staff Agencies for the Commandant.

RESOURCE EVALUATION AND ANALYSIS

The Resource Evaluation and Analysis (REA) function is designed to provide Commanders an in-house capability to examine, analyze, evaluate, and explore those areas of operations where known or potential problem areas exist which may adversely affect the efficient and economical use of financial resources. REA is an integral element of the command's financial management staff and is authorized at every command having a Comptroller. The REA function must be assigned to the Comptroller organization and will serve as the command focal point for external audits and internal controls. REA allow Commanders the opportunity to prepare for command IG inspections in advance. Commanders need to encourage maximum communication between command IG offices and REAs.

Effective use of REA will not only ensure a means for assessing the adequacy and quality of internal command operations, but will also serve as the basis for the timely detection and correction of conditions and practices. *MCO 7540.2E applies.*

MARINE CORPS ADMINISTRATIVE ANALYSIS TEAMS (MCAAT)

There are two permanent Administrative Analysis teams in the Marine Corps, one based at MCB Camp Pendleton and the other at MCB Camp Lejeune. These teams come under the operational control of HQMC (Code MI) and provide direct field representation. The teams provide Commanders and their staff education and instruction on Marine Corps policies and procedures that effect administration, pay, and allowances. They are designed to identify and assist in resolving problem areas in personnel administration and pay related management procedures and recommend actions, as may be necessary, for improvements in the administrative and financial functions inherent in Marine Corps organizations. They evaluate the effectiveness of systems, procedures, and internal controls relating to the proper and timely payment of appropriated military pay funds and ensures the best interest of the government and the individual Marine are protected.

MARINE CORPS FINANCIAL EVALUATION AND ANALYSIS TEAM (MCFEAT)

The mission of MCFEAT is to assess and evaluate financial management business practices and oversee financial management improvements to improve the accuracy and timeliness of recording and reporting financial information. They are a liaison between the Commanding Officer, Comptroller, and Defense Finance and Accounting Service (DFAS). They report to DC P&R (RFA) and have the following functions:

- Maintain Standard Financial Management Business Practices (SFMBP) template
- Develop financial management evaluation criteria
- Conduct financial management inspections
- Develop and recommend financial management improvement initiatives
- Recommend and implement financial management policies and procedures
- Advise P&R leadership on DFAS integration of system and business processes
- Supervise financial management business analyst in conducting process reviews and improvements
- Supervise Marine Corps Reserve Activation Travel Section (MCRATS)

MARINE CORPS FINANCIAL MANAGEMENT OPERATIONS SUPPORT (MCFMOS)

The mission of MCFMOS is to identify, document, and publish the root cause of problem transactions to Marine Corps commands in direct coordination with DFAS Cleveland (DFAS-CL). They perform reconciliation and analysis for all accounts payable, accounts receivable and payment transactions to improve the relevance, timeliness, and accuracy of financial transaction reporting. MCFMOS performs trend analysis and reports findings and recommendations that improve financial efficiency, internal controls, and execution of financial policy and training for all Marine Corps Major Command Recipients. They are a liaison between the Commanding Officer, Comptroller, and DFAS. MCFMOS reports to DC P&R (RFA).

CHAPTER IV

CONTRACTING & ACQUISITION

CONTRACTING SUPPLIES AND SERVICES

Knowledge of strengths and weaknesses of the contracting process will better equip Commanders to make legal purchases.

CONTRACTING ACTIVITIES

All products or services in the Marine Corps are procured by one of the following activities:

- Marine Corps Regional Contracting Offices (RCO) – supplies and services.
- Marine Corps Contracting Offices (limited authority) – supplies and services.
- Marine Corps Systems Command (MCSC) – Expeditionary Force weapons and IT system programs, as defined in SECNAVINST 5400.15C, Enclosure (5).
- Marine Corps Logistics Command (MCLC) – all ground weapon systems, secondary reparable items, and consumable items, as defined in MCO 4000.58.
- Naval Facilities Engineering Command (NAVFAC) (and in some theaters, U.S. Army Corps of Engineers) – all Military Construction (MILCON) Program projects and most facility related repair, maintenance and services.

CONTRACTING AUTHORITY LEVELS

In most cases within the Marine Corps, review and approval authority for formal contract actions resides with the contracting office. The Chief of Contracting Office (CCO) and Procuring Contracting Officer (PCO) generally serve as the final authorities up to $1M. Above that level of contract authority, HQMC (LB), Deputy Commandant, Installations and Logistics (DC I&L), and Deputy Assistant Secretary of the Navy (Acquisition and Logistics Management (DASN (A&LM)) involvement will be required.

ACQUISITION CYCLE

Acquisition plans should be formed early. There are many moving parts that need to be managed to make this process go smoothly, but a strong acquisition plan will provide the roadmap for smooth execution. The chart below shows typical Procurement Administrative Lead Time (PALT) for contracted products or services. Requesting activities should be involved with acquisition planning as soon as a requirement is identified. The contracting activity should also be included as part of the planning process.

Procurement Administrative Lead Time (PALT) GUIDELINES	
Estimated Purchase Request Cost	PALT
$1 - $9,999	Up to 12 days
$10,000 - $24,999	Up to 20 days
$25,000 - $99,999	Up to 35 days
$100,000 and over	3 – 9 months

Although local processes may vary, the basic acquisition cycle includes planning, solicitation, evaluation, award and post-award phases. Commanders are well served by having an overall acquisition strategy for managing the acquisition and fulfilling command requirements in a timely manner, and within budget. The strategy should address sources, type of contract, and funding. NOTE: Make sure the funding for the work to be performed is available before the solicitation phase.

BUYING GOODS AND SERVICES

Various types of procurements are designed to provide supplies or services at the best value and as quickly as possible. Procurements greater than $1 million are submitted to HQMC (LB) for pre-award review. Common purchases and procurement tools are listed below:

Simplified Purchases:

- Purchases less than $100,000
- Open market purchases of supplies or non-personal services
- Purchases made against an established contract or with government sources

Micro-Purchases:

- Purchases less than $3,000
- Other services less than $3,000, including small construction projects
- Use Government-wide Commercial Purchase Card (GCPC)
- Exempt from Small Business and Buy American Acts
- Justification required if not using GCPC for micro purchase

Purchase Orders:

- Purchases between $3,000 to $100,000
- Buy American Act applies
- All open market procurements are reserved for small businesses unless:
  o Ordering from intergovernmental agencies or pre-established contracts; or
  o Contracting Officer determines that quotes from two or more small businesses are unattainable in terms of market price, quality and delivery.

Blanket Purchase Agreement (BPA). A simplified method of procuring anticipated repetitive needs for supplies or services by establishing "ordering agreements" with qualified sources of supply.

PR Builder. PR Builder is a web-based mandatory-use system for submitting purchase requests. PR Builder (https://www.prbuilder.navy.mil) automates the process by which a Purchase Request (PR) will be generated and routed between the originator and the contracting communities. It includes fiscal approvals as well.

COMMAND PRIORITIES

Priority codes communicate the urgency of a requirement. The apparent tendency is for commands to assign high priority codes for goods and services to expedite shipment. The impact is that acquisition systems are overwhelmed with inaccurately prioritized items, and the warfighters do not always get what they need, when they need it. *Reference: MCO 4400.16G (Changes 1-3).*

Commanders should be honest brokers in priority assignments, and resist the temptation to game the system. If priority is truly "Urgent", the purchase request must have an Urgency Impact Statement (UIS) which must be on battalion letterhead, signed by the Commanding Officer, and annotate a specific delivery date (ASAP is not acceptable.)

CONTRACTING REGULATIONS/GUIDANCE:

- Federal Acquisition Regulation (FAR) – (http://www.arnet.gov/far)
- Defense Federal Acquisition Regulation Supplement (DFARS) – (http://www.acq.osd.mil/dpap/)
- Defense Acquisition Guidebook – (https://akss.dau.mil/dag/)
- DFARS Procedures Guidance and Information (PGI) – (http://www.acq.osd.mil/dpap/dars/dfarspgi/current/index.html)
- Navy Marine Corps Acquisition Regulation Supplement (NMCARS) – (http://acquisition.navy.mil/content/view/full/3464)
- Marine Corps Acquisition Procedures Supplement (MAPS) – applies to all USMC organizations receiving contracting authority from the DC I&L (LB). (See MAPS and other procurement policy and guidance links at http://www.marines.mil/units/hqmc/logistics/Pages/DivisionLBMain.aspx)
- Marine Corps Contract Management Process Guide (CMPG) – A web-enabled guide designed to benefit contracting personnel within the Marine Corps Field Contracting System (MCFCS) and their customers. The CMPG houses process and regulatory guidance, tools in the form of templates and samples, and hyperlinks to additional information to promote consistency and standardization across the field, reduce variation, and open communication channels across the MCFCS to share best practices and lessons learned. – (http://www.hqmc.usmc.mil/cmpg/)

WARFIGHTING REQUIREMENTS

Marine Corps Commanders have a mechanism in the acquisition process to identify improvements in warfighting capabilities which can benefit all Marines. Items identified for procurement to support contingency operations will be identified through the Universal Needs Statement (UNS) process as managed by the Marine Corps Combat Development Command (MCCDC). In this process, operating force units identify operational enhancement opportunities and deficiencies in capabilities, and submit an UNS to MCCDC for the required system or piece of equipment. During the review process for the UNS, the item will be identified as either centrally managed or non-centrally managed. If the item is centrally managed, it will be procured by MCSC using Procurement funds. MCO 3900.15B describes the UNS process in detail.

An UNS can be generated by an Advocate, the operating forces, or the supporting establishment. It is further developed by an Advocate to address required capabilities and transition a capability into a warfighting requirement. An UNS is forwarded to CG, MCCDC (Expeditionary Force Development Center (EFDC) Capabilities Assessment Branch) for entry into EFDS and registration into the Combat Development Tracking System (CDTS). The Combat Development Tracking System (CDTS) is available at the MCCDC website https://www.mccdc.usmc.mil. An UNS is assessed, reviewed, and validated. If the requirement is not valid, the UNS is returned to the originator with a non-concur endorsement. If validated, the UNS goes to a Doctrine, Organization, Training, Materiel, Leadership & Education, Personnel, and Facilities (DOTMLPF) Working Group for evaluation. The working group will develop specific solution courses of action. The result may be that the requirement gets incorporated into the Marine Corps POM process, and when resourced, gets fielded Marine Corps wide.

CHAPTER V

FREQUENTLY ASKED QUESTIONS (FAQs)

BASIC INFORMATION:

As a USMC Commander, what are my financial duties and responsibilities?

Commanders who receive funds from the CMC, a MARFOR, or an MSC (in other words, all Bn Commanders and above) must perform the following financial responsibilities:

- Prepare a financial plan.
- Use funds in accordance with approved plans and directives from higher authority.
- Prevent over commitment, over obligation, or over expensing of funds.
- Maintain oversight of budget reports to maintain awareness of available funds balance.
- Conduct continuous review of internal fiscal operations and related internal controls.
- Prevent unauthorized commitments of funds.
- Conduct command operations in the most cost effective manner to remain within administrative fund limitations made by the next higher echelon of command.
- Conduct continuous oversight of internal fiscal operations and related internal controls. (Chronic areas of concern are the Government-wide Commercial Purchase Card and ServMart cards. If not carefully monitored, both present ample opportunity for unauthorized or pilferable items.)
- Execute funds legally. For example: Do not use O&M to for a centrally managed program. Do not execute a minor construction project that exceeds the authorized monetary limit (currently $750,000). Do not purchase personal items with O&M.

References: MCO P7100.8K, MCO P7300.21A

What should my fiscal Marines be doing to support our fiscal mission?

Reconciliations, Validations, Tri-Annual Reviews and coordination with your Comptroller.

What are the limits on my financial authority?

If you receive less funding than you requested, you will need to revise your financial plans by effecting reductions in those programs which you consider to be least essential to the accomplishment of your overall mission.

Realignment of authorization between budget activities (for example, trying to move money between 1A1A Operating Forces funds to BSS1 Base Operations) is **not** authorized without prior HQMC approval. A basic fund limitation placed on Commanders consists of a new obligation authority limitation. This is a legal limitation imposed by Congress to the lowest organizational element granted an OPBUD or SUBOPBUD. It is subject to the Antideficiency Act, 31 U.S.C. 1517. In plain language, this means you can't obligate or spend more than you were authorized on your OPBUD.

Additionally, other specific limitations may be assigned regarding specific programs and funds. These funds are provided for stated purposes only and may not be used otherwise. Examples include:

- Flight operations
- Agricultural out-lease
- Recycling/Recycling proceeds
- Drugs and Counter-Narcotics programs
- Official Representation Funds (ORF)

In order to carry out these responsibilities effectively, Commanders must continually be aware of their current fiscal status and must know how funds are spent within their organization to accomplish operational objectives. They should be cognizant of fixed costs and costs required to perform normal recurring evolutions of an operational nature (e.g. preventive maintenance, training exercises, schools, etc.).

References: 31 U.S.C. 1517, MCO P7100.8K, MCO P7300.21A

What are my budget execution goals?

When you prepared your budget, you identified how much of your anticipated funding you expect to spend each month of the fiscal year. This submission then serves as the benchmark for execution by your higher headquarters. Variances should be communicated to your higher headquarters as soon as they become known to you. Severe over-execution can result in adverse administrative, legal or criminal repercussions. Severe under-execution can result in funds being withdrawn by higher headquarters.

What are my dollar value limits on execution?

Commanders are limited in the amount they can spend based on the dollar value they have been authorized. Each operating budget, allotment, and sub-allotment should be viewed as a checkbook account. Commanders do not have authority to exceed their allocations and 'bounce' checks.

References: 31 U.S.C. 1517, MCO P7100.8K, MCO P7300.21A

What is an unauthorized commitment?

An "unauthorized commitment" is defined in FAR 1.602-3(a) as "an agreement that is not binding solely because the Government representative who made it lacked the authority to enter into that agreement on behalf of the Government." **The only individuals who can bind the Government are warranted Contracting Officers and purchase cardholders acting within the limits of their delegated authority.** Unauthorized commitments violate federal law, federal regulation, and the Government-wide Standards of Conduct for Federal Employees.

Examples of unauthorized commitments include:

- Supplies or services are ordered by someone not named on a purchase card or identified in a contract or blanket purchase agreement. Note: A funding document is not a contractual document.

- A contractor starts work before the contractual document is issued or awarded by a Contracting Officer.
- An invoice is received from a contractor, but no purchase order or contract exists for the items or work described in the invoice.
- A purchase cardholder exceeds single purchase limitation without proper authorization/delegation of authority.

There are severe consequences for all parties involved with the unauthorized commitment. Unauthorized commitments may result in personal liability for the individual who made the commitment. Personnel responsible for unauthorized commitments are required to give detailed written explanations of their actions and may be subject to disciplinary action, especially if violations are flagrant and/or repetitive.

The process whereby designated individuals convert an unauthorized commitment to a legal contract is called ratification. Ratifications may only occur when all the regulatory requirements or conditions have been met. Contracting Officers do no have the authority to simply issue a purchase order or contract modification when an unauthorized commitment has been identified.

Contractors who act on unauthorized commitments do so at their own risk. They are not entitled to consideration (money) unless and until the unauthorized commitment is ratified. Payment is therefore substantially delayed or may not be forthcoming at all if the action is not ratified or costs are not recognized.

References: FAR, DFAR

What is my contracting authority?

Commanders at all levels have the same authority to initiate contracts, but the authority to approve contracts varies. A matrix detailing approval requirements, limits, and authorities is resident in MAPS. Requesting units only have the authority to purchase on their own, items that are $3,000 or less, via the Government-wide Commercial Purchase Card (GCPC). All other contract actions must be initiated via a Purchase Request (PR) submitted through PR Builder to the Regional Contracting Office (RCO). Under no circumstances should any direct arrangement be made between unit personnel and vendors without a contract being in place for purchases over $3,000. Likewise, splitting purchases in order to keep below the $3,000 single-purchase threshold will be viewed as an unauthorized commitment of funds requiring a retroactive contract ratification action.

References: FAR, DFAR, MAPS

What is MyPay?

DFAS has implemented significant improvements to payroll activities as part of the President's Management Agenda E-Government efforts. DFAS administers the MyPay payroll project. This web-based system delivers personal pay information, processes pay-related transactions in a timely, safe and secure manner, and allows access to electronic tax statements and other financial information online. The MyPay system allows DFAS customers to make changes directly to their own pay accounts in a secure electronic environment via a web site or via an interactive phone system. Members of America's armed forces, defense civilians, and military retirees and annuitants can make changes that previously required interaction with administrative staff and preparing paperwork. The MyPay system communicates with six different Department of Defense payroll and travel systems to support over five million customers including Marine Corps, Army, Navy, Air Force, Military Retirees, Civilians and Annuitants.

Reference: DoDFMR 7000.14-R

How are my civilians paid?

Civilian labor is normally the single, largest type of cost for bases and stations and a growing cost for the Operating Forces. The costs associated with labor are broken down into two categories, basic pay with other pay entitlements (i.e., overtime, shift, etc.), and fringe benefits (i.e., the government's share of retirement, Federal Insurance Contributions Act (FICA), health benefits, etc.).

There are two separate operations that are performed to account and keep track of labor hours and costs concerning civilian employees. The first operation is time and attendance and is performed primarily for payroll purposes. Time and attendance information is manually entered into the Defense Civilian Pay System (DCPS) or into the Standard Labor Data Collection and Distribution Application (SLDCADA) system, which will automatically feed DCPS. The second operation is labor distribution. Labor distribution is a cost accounting function that ensures that the costs associated with civilian labor are properly charged within the accounting system.

NAF employees are federal employees but are not civil servants. NAF employees are not legally part of the federal civil service; consequently, the policies, procedures, and entitlements relating to employees paid from appropriated funds and those relating to NAF employees are different. The Marine Corps has close to twelve thousand NAFI employees.

References: MCO 12790.2 W/CH1, MCO 12510.2C W/CH1, MCO P12000.11A

MISSION ACCOMPLISHMENT:

How do I request funds?

Commanders are responsible for determining operational objectives and formulating financial plans and budgets. Each command must determine their financial requirements, based on guidance received from the next higher echelon of command and past experience data. To request additional funds:

- Submit requirements in the format and in such detail as is prescribed by the next higher echelon of command.
- Examine mission requirements and assigned tasks to determine the most cost effective means by which they may be accomplished.
- Prepare budget estimates for accomplishing the mission and assigned tasks.
- Submit these budget estimates, accompanied by detailed justification, to the grantor of the funds.

References: MCO P7100.8K, MCO 7300.21A, MCO 7301.116 W/ERRATUM

What can we spend during a Continuing Resolution Authority period?

A Continuing Resolution Authority (CRA) is a Congressional action that provides budget authority for specific, ongoing activities when the regular fiscal year Appropriations Act has not been enacted. A continuing resolution usually specifies a maximum rate at which an agency may incur obligations and is based either on the prior year spending rate or a set percentage. A CRA allows commands to continue daily operations before authorizations have been passed down by HQMC. HQMC (P&R) will provide specific guidance upon approval of a CRA and on the limits commands are authorized. Normally, new starts are not authorized while under a CRA.

Reference: DoD FMR 7000.14-R

How should we 'manage' unfunded requirements?

It is incumbent upon Commanders and program sponsors to do everything to internally satisfy major unfunded requirements. Programmatic shortfalls should be addresses though the POM process which is the proper place to identify new programs or major increases to existing programs.

Since the POM process addresses 18 months out, interim funding may be needed to hold you over. In this regard, you should identify your year of execution shortfall to your higher headquarters as soon as they are known to you. At a minimum, they should be addressed during the mid year review. Once prioritized and inducted into the HQMC Current Year Deficiency (CYD) Database, these shortfalls will be considered as additional funds become available throughout the year.

Command inputs to the mid year review should include the following details:

- Identification of whether the requirement has/has not been approved by the POM or POM review.
- Documentation of the following:
    a) Who is requesting support?
    b) How much is the request?
    c) What the request will specifically fund?
    d) Why the request is being made?
    e) When is it needed?
    f) What is the funding line for prior year, current year, and future years?
    g) What is the impact if the request in not funded?

Commands submit funding requests with a cover letter addressing the Commander's concerns via the chain of command. If the MARFOR level cannot support, but concurs with the requirement, it should then be inducted into the CYD Database.

References: DoD FMR 7000.14-R, MCO 7301.116 W/ERRATUM

Why are Unliquidated Obligations (ULO) important?

ULOs represent wasted tax dollars and a loss of a Commander's financial resources. A Commander's efforts to make the most efficient use of resources cannot be accomplished without ensuring that the command's ULOs are effectively monitored. ULOs are those obligations issued for goods or services that have not been received or have been received but the bill has yet to be paid. Failure to review and de-obligate funds on INVALID obligations results in a lost opportunity to free up scarce funding, reduce your deficiency backlog, and improve your readiness. In addition, each year GAO conducts a review of unliquidated funding. The review is provided to Congress who uses it to mark us at the beginning of each fiscal year based on a 10 year analysis.

References: DoDFMR 7000.14-R

Why are Outstanding Travel Orders (OTO) Important?

DoD FMR, Volume 9 requires all travelers to file a voucher within five duty days after returning from TDY. All travel orders that have an estimated return date greater than five duty days are classified as Outstanding Travel Orders. These are similar to ULOs in that they represent wasted command funds in the event the traveler cancelled his TAD. It is the responsibility of your personnel administration office (consolidated admin or your G-1) to ensure OTO's are either settled or deobligated. Potential administrative issues artificially reduce the funds available to the command to accomplish its mission.

Why are Outstanding Travel Advances (OTA) important?

These are advances that were provided to that traveler, whose orders have become OTOs. As with ULOs and OTOs, OTAs represent wasted command funds in the event the traveler cancelled his TAD. As with OTOs, it is the responsibility of your personnel administration office to ensure OTA's result in either a settled travel claim or a pay checkage to the traveler. To control outstanding travel advances, your personnel administration office must reconcile on a monthly basis these records with the traveler who received the travel advance.

Why are outstanding commitments important?

These represent a document that may potentially result in an obligation. A commitment can take two courses. It either represents a valid obligation or an error that requires correction. Particularly during the end of the year, large commitments can jeopardize a Commander's financial account. If the commitments, coupled with the obligations, exceed the yearly authority, you are at significant risk of committing an ADA violation. If the commitments are invalid, then you risk potentially wasting funds that you could have directed to important operational requirements. To improve the accuracy of your available funds throughout the fiscal year, your fiscal Marines should periodically review outstanding commitments. Towards the last two months of the fiscal year, this review should be daily.

Why are Unmatched Disbursements (UMD) important?

A UMD is a disbursement transaction that has been received and accepted by an accounting activity, but has not been matched to an obligation. This includes both Disbursing Notification Records (DNR) and Interdepartmental Billings (IDB).

These represent liquidations that have no commitment or obligation of funds in the accounting system. Your fiscal officer must research this to determine whether one of the following three scenarios occurred:

1) The disbursement is valid and a valid obligation exists but either the obligation or the disbursement had an error in the line of accounting. In this instance the problem was fixed and you have a net zero impact to your account.
2) The disbursement is not valid to your account, in this instance the disbursement is removed and you have no impact to your account.
3) The disbursement is valid and you failed to record an obligation. In this instance your obligations will increase and your available balance will decrease. This is not a good scenario because there is a potential for committing an ADA violation.

Why are Negative Unliquidated Obligations (NULO's) important?

A NULO is a disbursement transaction that has been matched to the cited detail obligation, but the total disbursement exceeds the amount of the obligation. This could mean that more funds may have been spent than you know about. Your fiscal personnel should analyze this to find out whether the additional disbursements are valid. If they are, you need to increase your obligation to cover the liquidation – in this scenario, you risk an ADA violation. If the disbursement is not valid, then you need to identify the discrepancy to DFAS, via your chain of command so that the erroneous/duplicate disbursement can be corrected.

How can I get outside assistance for Financial Management?

Outside assistance is readily available to the Commander for Financial Management (FM) issues. The Comptroller organizations within each chain of command are available to conduct assist visits. Resource Evaluation and Analysis (REA) assist visits can be requested and they will perform a detailed FM assessment within the command.

Reference: MCO 7220.13G, MCO 7540.2E, MCO 7500.4A, MCO 7510.2E

APPROPRIATIONS/AUTHORIZATION FUNDING:

What are expiring funds?

Expiring funds are appropriations that cannot be carried over into the next fiscal year for new obligations. Those funds must be committed and obligated before the term of the appropriation expires otherwise they are lost. Similarly, reverted balances occur when invalid obligations are identified after the year concludes. When these invalid obligations are deobligated it exposes lost opportunities since these funds could have been reapplied to purchase other goods and services. In FY 2005, the USMC lost $70+M of lost purchasing power because of a lack of attention to the accounting records. These reverted funds could have funded the operations of a peacetime MEF for a full year.

Reference: DoDFMR 7000.14-R

When can funding execution cross fiscal years?

The Marine Corps is funded through many appropriations. The primary appropriations are classified into three types: one year (i.e., annual), multiple (i.e., more than one year), and no-year (i.e., continuing). The classification is determined by the period of time that the appropriation is available for obligations.

References: 31 U.S.C. 1502, MCO P7100.8K, MCO 7300.21A

What are my limits on Official Representation Funds (ORFs)?

Official Representation Funds (ORFs) shall be maintained at Flag officer level to host official receptions, dinners, and similar events, and to otherwise extend official courtesies to guests of the United States and the Department of Defense for the purpose of maintaining the standing and prestige of the United States and the Department of Defense. Generally, such events are hosted and official courtesies extended for:

- Civilian or military dignitaries and officials of foreign governments.
- Senior U.S. Government officials.
- Dignitaries and senior officials of state and local governments.
- Other distinguished and prominent citizens (may include retired or former civilian or military officials of the Department) who have made a substantial contribution to the United States or the Department of Defense.

Commanders must request ORF funds from the Assistant for Administration to the Under Secretary of the Navy (AAUSN), via their chain of command, by August for the next execution period 1 Oct to 30 Sept. Commanders receive their allocation by letter which identifies their funding ceiling. AAUSN provides additional funding on a prioritized, as available basis. Commanders need to identify emerging requirements to higher headquarters as soon as possible. There is no guarantee of additional funding. ORF functions must meet certain non-DoD guest ratios. *Less than 30 persons = at least 20% non-DoD; 30 persons or more = at least 50% non-DoD.*

Gifts/mementos funded with ORF must have a command or official theme and not be personal in nature. Aggregate cost of gift and mementos presented by a DoD Official to an authorized guest may not exceed $305. Currently, mementos presented to high-ranking DoD officials on official visits to field activities are limited to value of less than $40.00. Medallions/coins purchased with ORF, for example, may only be given to hosted guests. They cannot be given to Marines or civilian employees. Below are unauthorized uses of ORF funds:

- To pay for the cost of meals or refreshments for U.S. Government employees in connection with routine interagency or intra-agency working meetings.
- To pay for purely social events intended primarily for the entertainment or benefit of DoD officials and employees, their families, or personal guests.
- To pay expenses for official courtesies that are minimally required to host select DoD officials (listed in DoDD 7250.13, February 17, 2004) when they are on official visits to the field. Details on the specific expenses that can be paid with ORF are included in the DoD Directive cited below.

Commanders must monitor ORF expenditures closely to ensure that each expenditure was made for officially hosted functions in connection with official events which comply with socially acceptable mores of American society. ORF must serve the policy objectives of the United States and the interests of the U.S. taxpayer jointly.

Commanders must maintain the records on the use of ORF on a function-by-function basis to provide data on the "how's" and "why's" of funds usage. For example, records should document the purpose for which funds were used including names, titles, and the organizations of the persons attending.

References: SECNAVINST 7042.7K, DoDD 7250.13

PROCEDURAL DOs & DON'Ts

How does the Marine Corps fund contingency operations?

Contingency operations for emergent mission requirements are often funded after-the-fact by supplemental appropriations issued by Congress. Initially, field commanders may have to reprioritize their O&M budgets to carry out contingency operations. Commanders must track and report the 'cost' of contingency operations so HQMC can make detailed requests to Congress for reimbursement.

Commanders must develop detailed financial plans to request reimbursement of incremental costs incurred above baseline funding.

During Humanitarian Assistance/Disaster Relief (HA/DR) missions, commands must have specific authorization to give away U.S. stores of equipment or consumables directly to other governments, military, Non-Governmental Organizations or victims. This authority to use O&M funds is limited and must be specifically authorized in order to be reimbursed by Overseas Humanitarian Disaster and Civic Aid (OHDACA) funding, which is generally authorized as part of a deployment order (DEPORD)

References: DoD FMR 7000.14R, MARADMIN 133/02, 10 U.S.C. 40, Joint Pub 1-06

Why do I need to do a reimbursable?

DoD activities may furnish the sale of material, work, and services to other DoD components or public sources on a reimbursable basis pursuant to public laws and DoD policies. There are two types of reimbursable orders: Economy Act orders and Project Orders, which can further be broken down into funded or unfunded reimbursable.

Economy Act Orders are normally used for work or services of a normal or recurring nature (e.g., utility support, administrative support, janitorial support, etc.), as well as one time work orders and Project Orders are normally used for work or services with long completion times or for non-recurring types of work, such as a construction project.

Reference: DoD FMR 7000.14R

How do we pay for reimbursables with other DoD service / agency support?

The Military Interdepartmental Purchase Request (MIPR) form, DD 448, authorizes funds for an external command, outside the DON, to perform work or services for the requesting command. For example, if a Marine unit is training at an Army base, the Marine unit will send funds to the Army Base Comptroller with the MIPR to fund work or services required by the Marine unit. However, MIPR's require a Determination and Finding (D&F) to justify why the work should be done outside of the Marine Corps. The RCO can assist you in providing the required documentation and approval process for the D&F. In many cases where a re-occurring requirement has identified one Service as an Executive Agent for providing support services, there may be a blanket D&F already in existence.

References: FAR, DFAR, MAPS

How do we pay for assisted acquisitions outside DoD?

What about assisted acquisitions using Economy Act and Non-Economy Act orders placed with agencies outside the DoD?

Executing a reimbursable agreement between two DoD agencies (e.g. Marine Corps and Army) usually results in few problems other than ensuring we return funds in a timely manner back to the other service if we are accepting a reimbursable (to prevent reversions to them) or ensuring we properly closeout our reimbursables at the end of the year to ensure we don't over obligate or revert funds after the fiscal year closes.

The bigger issue is when we place orders with agencies outside the Marine Corps. Controls need to be in place to prevent violations of the ADA. One of those controls is the mandatory requirement to produce a Determination and Finding (D&F). The D&F is to assure that use of the other agency is in the best interest of the Marine Corps. The development of a D&F is a cumbersome process intended to prevent ADA violations as well as violations of the Federal Acquisition Regulations and DoD policy. This process was imposed due to rampant abuse of orders placed with other agencies.

References: MAPS, CMC ltr lb/pr 4200 dtd 11 May 07

What do I need to know about the Government Travel Charge Card Program (GTCCP)?

The GTCCP facilitates official travel. The Commander's Personnel Administrators (consolidated administrators) and the AC/S, G-1 owns the official travel business process. Charges incurred on the GTCCP are personal in nature and not related to an appropriation. Commanders, through their AC/S, G-1, remain responsible for the execution and monthly review of the GTCCP within their commands. A Commanders Agency Program Coordinator (APC), typically their AC/S, G-1 or their Personnel Officer, provides oversight of the GTCCP. A successful program is one with no delinquent cardholders. APC duties include:

- Assist and educate cardholders on GTCCP issues
- Hold individual cardholders responsible to pay their GTCCP bill whether they have been reimbursed for their travel or not
- Proactively work reports and report delinquency and misuse to the Commander/supervisor
- Brief the Commander monthly on GTCCP issues

Reference: MCO 4600.40A

What do I need to know about the Government Commercial Purchase Card?

The Government-wide Commercial Purchase Card Program (GCPC), also known as the Purchase Card, has proven to be a successful procurement tool. ADC I&L (LB) provides Marine Corps policy for use of the GCPC as a method of payment for actions over $2,500, and established policy for use of the GCPC as a method of payment. To obtain a waiver to this policy, cardholders must obtain approval from the head of the Regional Contracting Office (RCO), or their designee, to use the GCPC as the method of payment for purchases above $2,500 for services, $3,000 for supplies, and below $25,000. Use of the GCPC as the method of payment for purchases of $25,000 or more requires approval by HQMC, I&L (LB).

When using the GCPC with Government sources of supply or as a method of payment for simplified acquisitions and electronic orders placed against competed Indefinite Delivery Indefinite Quantity (IDIQ) contracts, the threshold is $100,000 ($5.5 million for commercial items including options, using the procedures of FAR Part 13.5, and $9,999,900 for orders issued against GSA schedule contracts or other Indefinite Delivery Contracts (IDCs).

Because the GCPC is easy to use, Commanders need to pay particular attention to its use. The GCPC has an inherently high risk of being abused to buy unauthorized or pilferable items. A Commander's GCPC cardholder needs adequate oversight and supervision to ensure items purchased are requested and approved by someone other than the cardholder. Further, Commanders must ensure due diligence by ensuring receipts match to the GCPC purchase requests. This ensures cardholder do not do "window-shopping".

The APC, generally located at the Regional Contracting Office (RCO), manages the program for the Commanding Officer. APC responsibilities includes: establish purchase card accounts, provide training, delegate contracting authority, monitor and approve monthly GCPC statements conduct audits, and coordinate with the cardholders, the cardholders' command, and the GCPC bank.

References: Public Law 107-248 8149C, DoD GCPC Guidebook, NAVSUPINST 4200.99, MCBul 4400 series, MARADMIN 433/02, MARADMIN 628/00,

Can I buy command medallions ("coins")?

Medallions may be purchased with locally available appropriated funds and presented as awards for significant accomplishments. General Officers in command must authorize any purchase and use of these medallions ("coins") to recognize accomplishments as part of an official awards program, as spelled out in a Command Awards Order. Commands need to be aware of the limitations that apply to the giving of government funded coins.

- Do not use coins as a personal gift.
- Do not use coins as a token of appreciation.
- Do not use coins for recognition of the contributions of unaffiliated parties.
- Do not use coins to recognize volunteers unless specifically provided for by regulation.
- Refer to the ORF section for rules/regulations about coins purchased with ORFs
- Do ensure the command's name is on the coin
- Do not allow the coin to have the name of an individual Commander
- Do ensure the coin clearly states "For Excellence" or other verbiage making it clear the coin is an award and not a "remember me" memento
- Do ensure Commanders purchase only enough coins to meet the estimated needs for each fiscal year to prevent a bona fide needs statute violation.

Commanders must ensure they can track each coin's funding source. Commanders typically assign this duty to their Aide de Camp or Protocol office. As a reminder, coins purchased with Official Representation Funds (ORF) may only be given to official hosted guests. They cannot be given to Marines or civilian employees.

Absent an official awards program, distributing coins is considered a gift and this is not a permissible practice. Coins and medallions may, however, be purchased with personal funds. If a Commander's personal funds are used, he may use the coins in any manner he chooses. Because most coins require a substantial up-front minting cost and normally a minimum minting quantity, care must be taken to ensure the purchase is appropriate, in sufficient estimated quantity to not exceed current fiscal year requirements, and not co-mingled with other coins or mementos.

Reference: MCO 7042.6C

How do I fund conferences?

Financial responsibility for planning and conducting Marine Corps sponsored conferences lies with the sponsoring Commander or sponsoring staff agency head. Officials sponsoring a conference must exercise good stewardship of Marine Corps resources by ensuring that conference costs are minimized, best value is obtained by the Government, and that attendee conference travel expenses stay within normal per diem rates. Off-site conferences should be conducted only if a comparison with available DoD conference sites/lodging confirms the off-site location is comparable in price with DoD/MCCS-run facilities. Use of premium lodging sites should be avoided. While an ocean view or a 5-star golf course seems appealing, especially when spouses are also in attendance, they are not cost-effective and can (and have) result in hotline and other complaints. A Commander cannot collect attendee conference fees to offset the cost of the conference. Further, a Commander cannot reimburse or supplement the appropriation from which the conference is funded. A Commander also cannot authorize the use of appropriated funds to pay for an employee's food and light refreshments – this is funded through the employees travel voucher as is any conference fees charged by a non-DON conference sponsor.

Reference: MCO 7300.22A

How do we buy computers, IT equipment?

The general rule is that local command expense funds (O&M) may be used for IT purchases (to include non-NMCI desktops, laptops and servers) if the item(s) are not centrally managed or part of a centrally managed system, the total purchase (to include hardware, software and peripherals) is less than the expense/investment threshold (currently $250,000), or if the total purchase is $250,000 or more and the items do not comprise a "system" or improve system performance. Since purchases occasionally fall into a gray area under the fiscal definition of "'system", final determination of funding type will be made by HQMC P&R through the IT Procurement Request Review/Approval System (ITPRAS).

MCSC administers all centrally managed programs for the Marine Corps and is required to use PMC funds to procure centrally managed IT equipment, software, and peripherals. MCSC also develops and maintains Blanket Purchase Agreements (BPA) (equipment including desktops, laptops, servers, and storage devices) and Enterprise Agreements (EA) (software) to standardize IT and simplify the portfolio. Units using local O&M funds will procure information technology hardware and software from MCSC. MCSC will centrally procure IT hardware and software; such procurements will result in locally-managed assets that will be supported within the terms of the contract, BPA or EA. These assets will not be centrally refreshed which means that units must develop their own refresh schedule and adjust their future year budgets to accommodate refresh in the future.

All IT requirements (to include computers, software, servers, handheld radios, etc) must be coordinated with your AC/S, G-6 and your local Area Counsel Office. Each unit/command will have a designated coordinator that has the authority to approve requests under $25,000 that do not meet the special circumstances. All requests greater than $25,000 are reviewed and approved by HQMC. Local coordinators are guided by the following principles:

- Determine whether the IT products or services to be procured are covered under the NMCI contract and will be used primarily on the NMCI network or computers.
- Assess operational impact if purchases are postponed to allow NMCI to meet the requirement. This would be done when NMCI has the procurement of the requirement in their contract.
- Determine whether the proposed procurement is a valid operational or program requirement if not covered in the NMCI contract.
- Approve and forward a procurement request after ensuring it does not violate policies in the active references.

Commanders do not require ITPRAS approval for consumables such as paper, toner, floppy disks, or writeable/rewriteable CDs/DVDs.

Commanders do require ITPRAS approval for hard disk drives and thumb drives since they are not considered to be consumables. Copies of all current policy documents are located at: https://hqdod.hqmc.usmc.mil/itproc.asp

Bottom line: IT and communication purchases are the leading causes for breaking the law. Commanders should use their Comptroller and their Area Counsel Office to determine the legal use of funds.

Reference: DoD FMR 7000.14R, MARADMIN 363/05, MARADMIN 530/05, MARADMIN 486/06, MARADMIN 298/08, MARADMIN 591/08

What Can I do to pay for the Annual Marine Corps Birthday Ball?

Commanders can use O&M funds for the following expenses in support of the official ceremony:

- Security
- Official transportation
- Photography of the official ceremony
- Printing and publications supporting only the official ceremony
- Audio/visual support for the official ceremony

Commanders cannot use O&M funds for the social event. The social event includes the dinner, refreshments, favors, entertainment and other social activities. These functions shall be supported primarily through ticket sales, unit fundraising events (earned monies), unsolicited donations, and MCCS NAF or MWR APF, if available.

Fundraising for the Birthday Ball must comply with applicable guidance, to include the Joint Ethics Regulation. Commands CANNOT fundraise or secure commercial sponsorship for any purpose, including a Birthday Ball social event, since commands are funded with APF and the Antideficiency Act prohibits the augmentation of these funds. While commands CANNOT fundraise or enter into commercial sponsorship agreements, they may officially support fundraising in certain cases. Individual units may hold fundraising events to augment their own MCCS unit funds, but may not enter into commercial sponsorship agreement to augment their unit funds. Commercial sponsorship arrangements are not considered fundraising events, however, they may only be entered into by MCCS. For more guidance on fundraising, please contact your local Staff Judge Advocate or Area Counsel Office.

Reference: 10 U.S.C. 5042, DoDI 1015.15, MCO 7040.11A, MARADMIN 439/08

I have a big purchase that would be much more convenient if I broke it down into parts that are each less than $3K so I can use the GCPC to make the purchases, is this OK?

No, this is illegal. Do not fragment or piecemeal an acquisition merely to avoid exceeding the $3K ceiling, even if a case can be made for dividing the requirement. This constitutes a violation of the Purpose Statute, and will result in a violation of the Antideficiency Act. Consolidate similar type items into one order. Commanders must forward all requirements that exceed $3K to the Contracting Officer for procurement action.

Can I buy Business Cards?

Commanders can only use appropriated funds to purchase card stock and printer ink. They cannot use a commercial vendor to prepare the cards. Commanders must use in-house computing resources to print their own business cards. Only recruiters and criminal investigators can purchase commercially prepared business cards.

Reference: DoD Directive 5330.3

Can I buy civilian clothes so my Marines don't embarrass the command and are able to present a professional military presence when acting as an "ambassador of the Corps" in local or foreign destinations?

Commander's are authorized to provide cash allowances for civilian clothing to their enlisted Marines after detailing the requirements to and receiving approval from the Marine Corps Uniform Board per MCBul 10120. However, making a Marine look good for liberty does not constitute adequate justification.

Reference: MCBul 10120, MCO P10120.28G, MCO 10120.59A W/CH 1

My Marines are in the field, can I use O&M to purchase water?

The purchase of special drinking (i.e., bottle water, etc.) is generally a prohibited expenditure of O&M. An exception exists when:

1) The public water is unsafe for human consumption.
2) There is an emergency failure of water source on the installation.
3) There is a temporary facility with no drinking water available within a reasonable distance.

4) There is no water fit for drinking purposes available without cost or at a lower cost to the government.

References: <u>GAO Decisions</u>: A-97419 September 20, 1938; B-236330, August 14, 1989; B-303920, Mar. 21, 2006; B-310502, February 4, 2008

Can I use my O&M to provide coffee and donuts for my official meetings?

NO. GAO has published an opinion specifically determining coffee and donuts to be an unauthorized expense. Buying food for individual employees – at least those who are not away from their official duty station on travel status – does not materially contribute to an agency's mission performance. As a result, food is generally considered a personal expense.

References: GAO Decisions: B-163764, May 17, 1968; B-159633, May 20, 1974; B-233807 August 27, 1990; B-301184, Jan. 15, 2004; MCO 7300.22A

A Marine received a fine while in an official duty in a personal vehicle (or a government owned vehicle), can I use APF to pay for it?

Marines and civilian employees must pay their own fines regardless of whether the vehicle was privately or government owned. The payment of a fine or penalty does not materially contribute towards an agency's mission accomplishment so the use of a Commander's fund is not authorized.

References: GAO Decisions: B-231981, May 19, 1989, B-58378, 31 July 1978; B-102829, 8 May 1951; B173660, 18 November 1971; B205438, 12 November 1981; B-186680, 4 October 1976; B-191747, 6 June 1978; B-227388, 3 September 1987; B-161457, 9 May 1978

Can I use the Unit GCPC to place a deposit for a good or service?

The use of the purchase card or convenience check for the payment of "Deposits" is prohibited. A payment of this type is considered an advance payment, which is prohibited. Please refer to DC I&L (LB) for additional guidance.

What is Business Process Improvement (BPI)?

In an effort to improve management and efficiency, DoD established the Defense Business Transformation Agency to consolidate and transform the management of core business activities such as financial, property, and support services. This agency develops enterprise-wide business processes and use better information technology to increase the visibility over DoD assets, eliminate organizational barriers to efficiency, and enable more effective defense business systems operations. For more information on BPI, contact the Marine Corps Business Enterprise Office (MCBEO), DC I&L (LR).

APPENDIX A

ACRONYM GLOSSARY

AAUSN – Assistant for Administration to the Under Secretary of the Navy
ADA – Antideficiency Act
ADC – Assistant Deputy Commandant
AP – Acquisition Plan
APC – Agency Program Coordinator
APF – Appropriated Funds
APN – Aircraft Procurement, Navy
ARI – Allotment Recipient Identifier
ASN (FM&C) – Assistant Secretary of the Navy (Financial Management & Comptroller)
BEA – Budget Execution Activity
BEIS – Business Enterprise Information System
BESA – Budget Execution Sub-activity
BPA – Blanket Purchase Agreement
BPI – Business Process Improvement
CCO – Chief of Contracting Office
CDP – Combat Development Process
CDTS – Combat Development Tracking System
CG – Commanding General
CMC – Commandant of the Marine Corps
CMP – Centrally Managed Program
CMPG – Contract Management Process Guide
CNA – Center for Naval Analysis
CO – Commanding Officer
CONUS – Continental United States
CPG – Commandant's Planning Guidance
CRA – Continuing Resolution Authority
CYD – Current Year Deficiency
D&F – Determinations & Findings
DASN – Deputy Assistant Secretary of the Navy
DASN (ACQ) – Deputy Assistant Secretary of the Navy (Acquisition Management)
DASN (A&LM) – Deputy Assistant Secretary of the Navy (Acquisition & Logistics Management)
DC – Deputy Commandant
DCAA – Defense Contract Audit Agency
DCPS – Defense Civilian Pay System
DECC STL – Defense Enterprise Computing Center St. Louis
DEPORD – Deployment Order
DFAR – Defense Federal Acquisition Regulations
DFARS – Defense Federal Acquisition Regulation Supplement
DFAS – Defense Finance and Accounting System
DMA – Depot Maintenance Activity
DMAIC – Define, Measure, Analyze, Improve, Control
DMC – Defense Management Council
DMOC – Defense Management Oversight Committee
DoD – Department of Defense
DoDIG – Department of Defense Inspector General
DON – Department of Navy
DONPG – Department of Navy Programming Guidance
DOTMLPF – Doctrine, Organization, Training, Materiel, Leadership & Education, Personnel & Facilities
DPAG – Defense Planning Advisory Group

DPG – Defense Planning Guidance
DTS – Defense Transportation System
EA – Enterprise Agreement
EA – Executive Agent
EFDC – Expeditionary Force Development Center
ESG – Executive Steering Group
FAQ – Frequently Asked Question
FAR – Federal Acquisition Regulations
FFP – Firm Fixed Price
FHNMC – Family Housing, Navy and Marine Corps
FICA – Federal Insurance Contributions Act
FM – Financial Management
FMF – Fleet Marine Force
FMPM – Financial Management Policy Manual
FMR – Financial Management Regulation
FSS – Federal Supply Schedules
FTE – Full Time Equivalent
FYDP – Future Years Defense Plan
G&A – General and Administrative
GAO – Government Accountability Office
GCPC – Government Commercial Purchase Card
GO – General Officer
GSA – General Services Administration
GTCCP – Government Travel Charge Card Program
GWOT – Global War on Terror
HAC S&IS – House Appropriations Committee Surveys and Investigations Staff
HA/DR – Humanitarian Assistance/Disaster Relief
HQMC – Headquarters Marine Corps
I&L – Installations and Logistics
ICOFR – Internal Controls Over Financial Reporting
ICP – Internal Control Program
ICR – Internal Control Review
IDC – Indefinite Delivery Contracts
IDIQ – Indefinite Delivery, Indefinite Quantity
IR3B – Integrated Resource & Requirements Review Board
IT – Information Technology
ITPRAS – Information Technology Procurement Request Review/Approval System
J&A – Justification and Approval
JCS – Joint Chiefs of Staff
JMA/SA – Joint Mission Area/Support Area
JROC – Joint Requirements Oversight Council
LSS – Lean Six Sigma
MAPS – Marine Corps Acquisition Procedure Supplement
MAS – Multiple Award Schedules
MARADMIN – Marine Administrative Message
MCAAT – Marine Corps Administrative Analysis Teams
MCBEO – Marine Corps Business Enterprise Office
MCCDC – Marine Corps Combat Development Command
MCCS – Marine Corps Community Services
MCFCS – Marine Corps Field Contracting System
MCFEAT – Marine Corps Financial Evaluation and Analysis Team
MCFMOS – Marine Corps Financial Management Operations Support
MCHS – Marine Corps Common Hardware Suite

MCLC – Marine Corps Logistics Command
MCMIC – Marine Corps Managers' Internal Control Program
MCMP – Marine Corps Master Plan
MCNAFAS – Marine Corps Nonappropriated Fund Audit Service
MCNR – Military Construction, Naval Reserve
MCO – Marine Corps Order
MCPIA – Marine Corps Productivity Improvement Account
MCSC – Marine Corps System Command
MCTFS – Marine Corps Total Force System
MEF – Marine Expeditionary Force
MIC – Managers' Internal Control Plan
MILCON – Military Construction, Navy
MILSTRIP – Military Standard Requisitioning & Issuing Procedures
MIPR – Military Interdepartmental Purchase Request
MLG – Marine Logistics Group
MOA – Memorandum of Agreement
MOPAS – Management and Oversight Process for the Acquisition of Services
MPMC – Military Personnel, Marine Corps
MPN – Military Personnel, Navy
MRI – Major Command Recipients
MROC – Marine Requirements Oversight Council
MWR – Morale, Welfare and Recreation
NAF – Non-Appropriated Funds
NAFI – Non-Appropriated Fund Instrumentalities
NAS – Naval Audit Service
NAVCOMPT – Navy Comptroller
NAVFAC – Naval Facilities Engineering Command
NMCAG – Navy Marine Corps Acquisition Guide
NMCARS – Navy Marine Corps Acquisition Regulation Supplement
NMCI – Navy Marine Corps Internet
NOA – New Obligation Authority
NULO – Negative Unliquidated Obligation
NWCF – Navy Working Capital Fund
O&MMC – Operation and Maintenance, Marine Corps
O&MMCR – Operation and Maintenance, Marine Corps Reserve
O&MN – Operations and Maintenance, Navy
O&MNR – Operations and Maintenance, Navy Reserve
OCONUS – Out of the Continental United States
OHDACA – Overseas Humanitarian Disaster and Civic Aid
OIF – Operation Iraqi Freedom
OMB – Office of Management and Budget
OMIC – Overall Managers' Internal Control Process
OPBUD – Operating Budget
OPN – Other Procurement, Navy
OPNAV – Office of the Chief of Naval Operations
ORF – Official Representation Funds
OSD – Office of the Secretary of Defense
OTA – Outstanding Travel Advances
OTO – Outstanding Travel Orders
P&R – Programs and Resources
PALT – Procurement Administrative Lead Time
PANMC – Procurement of Ammunition, Navy and Marine Corps
PCO – Procuring Contracting Officer

PEB – Program Evaluation Board
PGI – Procedure Guidance Information
PMC – Procurement, Marine Corps
POM – Program Objective Memoranda
POTUS – President of the United States
PPBES – Planning, Programming, Budget, Execution System
PR – Purchase Request
PRG – Program Review Group
PWG – Program Objective Memorandum Working Group
PWO – Public Works Officer
RCO – Regional Contracting Office
RDT&E, N – Research, Development, Test and Evaluation, Navy
REA – Resource Evaluation and Analysis
ROI – Return on Investment
ROTC – Reserve Officer Training Corps
RPA – Program Assessment Branch
RPMC – Reserve Personnel, Marine Corps
SABRS – Standard Accounting, Budgeting, and Reporting System
SECDEF – Secretary of Defense
SECNAV – Secretary of the Navy
SECNAVINST – Secretary of the Navy Instruction
SES – Senior Executive Service
SFMBP – Standard Financial Management Business Practices
SLDCADA – Standard Labor Data Collection and Distribution Application
SMARTS – Management Analytical Retrieval Tools System
SOA – Statement of Assurance
SPG – Strategic Planning Guidance
SRI – Suballotment Recipient Identifier
SRP – Smart Range Portal
SSP – Source Selection Plan
SUBOPBUD - Sub-Operating Budget
T&M – Time and Materials
TCP/IP – Transmission Control Protocol/Internet Protocol
TLCM – Total Life Cycle Management
TOA – Total Obligation Authority
U&FRF – Unit and Family Readiness Funds
UIS – Urgency Impact Statement
ULO – Unliquidated Obligations
UMD – Unmatched Disbursements
UNS – Universal Needs Statement
UPL – Unfunded Program List
USACE – U.S. Army Corps of Engineers
U.S.C. – United States Code
WCF – Working Capital Fund
WCI – Work Center Identifier

APPENDIX B

USMC FINANCIAL MANAGEMENT MARINE CORPS ORDERS

Short Title	Long Title
MCO 7000.19 W/CH 1	Marine Corps Nonappropriated Fund (NAF) Investment Policy
MCO 7010.17A	Religious Offering Fund (ROF)
MCO 7020.8D	Nonappropriated Fund International Balance Of Payments
MCO 7042.6C	Award Of Trophies And Similar Devices In Recognition
MCO 7110R.3F W/CH 1	Budgeting And Reporting Of Marine Corps Reserve Clothing
MCO 7130.1J W/CH 1	Issuance/Modification Of Permanent Change Of Station (PCS)
MCO 7220R.38C	Selected Reserve Incentive Program (SRIP)
MCO 7220.12P	Special Duty Assignment (SDA) Pay Program
MCO 7220.13G	Marine Corps Administrative Analysis Team (MCAAT) Program
MCO 7220.21E	Advance Pay Incident To A Permanent Change Of Station (PCS)
MCO 7220.24M	Selective Reenlistment Bonus (SRB) Program
MCO 7220.36A	Special Pay For Duty At Certain Places
MCO 7220.39D	Standard/Flat Rate Per Diem Allowances
MCO 7220.43B	Financial Assistance Program (FAP)
MCO 7220.44A	Marine Corps Policy For Paying Marines Under The Joint
MCO 7220.49A	Deductions From Pay For Delinquent Debts Owned
MCO 7220.50B	Marine Corps Policy For Paying Reserve Marines
MCO 7220.52E	Foreign Language Proficiency Pay (FLPP) Program
MCO 7220.54	Repayment Of Navy Relief Society (NRS) Loans Upon Separation
MCO 7240.3E	Abstraction Of Public Vouchers By Marine Corps Disbursing
MCO 7300.16B	Backup Data Sheet For Defense Business Operations Fund
MCO 7300.22A	Controlling Conference Costs
MCO 7301R.65	Fund Code System
MCO 7301.109	Policy For Funding Subordinate Commands
MCO 7301.112	Accounting For Collections Of Family Housing Receipts
MCO 7301.116 W/ERRATUM	Financial Management Of Unfunded Reimbursable Programs
MCO 7330.2B	Reporting Of Marine Corps Resources In Support of The U.S.
MCO 7500.4A	Command Investigation And Reporting Of Actual Or Apparent
MCO 7510.2E	Internal Audit Of Nonappropriated Fund Instrumentalities
MCO 7510.3E	Command Attention, Response And Follow-up To Audit Reports
MCO 7540.2E	Resource Evaluation And Analysis (REA) Function
MCO P7000.14K	Marine Corps Cost Factors Manual
MCO P7010.20	Marine Corps Community Services Nonappropriated Fund
MCO P7100.11 W/CH 1	Budget Manual For HQMC And Special Activities
MCO P7100.8K	Field Budget Guidance Manual
MCO P7300.19B	Marine Aircraft Group (MAG) Fiscal Handbook
MCO P7300.21A	Marine Corps Financial Execution Standard Operating
MCO P7301.104 W/CH 1 THRU 9	Accounting Under The Appropriations "Military Personnel,
NAVMC 2664	Financial Guidebook For Commanders

APPENDIX C

USEFUL WEB LINKS

Defense Finance and Accounting Service DFAS: www.dod.mil/dfas
- In 1991, the Secretary of Defense created the Defense Finance and Accounting Service to reduce the cost of Defense Department finance and accounting operations and to strengthen financial management through consolidation of finance and accounting activities across the department.

DoD Financial Management Regulation (FMR) (DoD 7000.14-R):
http://www.defenselink.mil/comptroller/fmr/
- This site provides financial management policy and procedures for the Department of Defense, in areas of general financial management, budget presentation, budget execution, accounting, disbursing, reporting, military pay, civilian pay, travel, contract payment, reimbursable operations, special accounts funds and programs, non-appropriated funds, administrative control of appropriations, and security assistance.

DoD Directives: http://www.dtic.mil/whs/directives
- The DoD Directives System was established to provide a single, uniform system of DoD issuances and directive-type memorandums used to convey DoD policies, responsibilities, and procedures. The DoD Directives System provides for the orderly processing, approval, publication, distribution, internal review, and records management of DoD Directives, DoD Instructions, and DoD Publications. The DoD Directives System also includes the Office of the Secretary of Defense (OSD) Federal Register System.

HQMC Programs and Resources (P&R): http://www.marines.mil/units/hqmc/pandr/Pages/default.aspx
- The Programs and Resources Department is the principal staff agency responsible to the Commandant of the Marine Corps for developing and defending the Marine Corps financial requirements, policies, and programs. The Deputy Commandant (DC) P&R owns the Marine Corps resource allocation process and serves as the principal adviser to the Commandant on all financial matters.

HQMC Audit & Review Branch (RFR): http://www.usmc.mil/units/hqmc/pandr/Pages/rfr.aspx
- HQMC Audit & Review Branch provides the Commandant of the Marine Corps, Deputy Commandant for Programs & Resources, and the Director, Fiscal Division with "honest broker" focused Marine Corps-wide liaison, oversight and tracking of external audits, internal controls, Antideficiency Act compliance and reporting, and banking/credit union programs.

HOMC Accounting and Financial Assistance Branch (RFA):
http://www.usmc.mil/units/hqmc/pandr/Pages/rfa.aspx
- HQMC Accounting and Financial Assistance Branch is a center of financial management excellence and quality in the review, analysis, and reporting of financial execution. RFA mission is to advise and assist the program sponsors, HQMC staff offices, and Marine Corps field comptrollers in all matters relating to accounting, related information systems, and program execution through on-going review and analysis.

Navy Financial Management: http://www.finance.hq.navy.mil
- Home page for Assistant Secretary of the Navy for Financial Management and Comptroller (ASN(FM&C))

Navy Directives: http://doni.daps.dla.mil/default.aspx
- Digital collection of all unclassified issuances released by the Secretary of the Navy and Chief of the Naval Operations. To find an instruction by number, navigate to either All Instructions or SECNAV or OPNAV. The SECNAV Instruction 7000.27A, for example, is found by clicking SECNAV from the Instructions drop-down menu, then the folder 07000, then the subfolder 07-00.

APPENDIX D

OTHER SUGGESTED LINKS

Acquisition, Technology, & Logistics (AT&L) http://www.acq.osd.mil

Central Contractor Register http://www.ccr.gov/

Defense FAR Supplement (DFARS) http://www.acq.osd.mil/dpap/

Defense Finance and Accounting Service (DFAS) http://www.dfas.mil

Defense Logistics Agency http://www.dla.mil

DoD http://www.defenselink.mil/

DoD Business Opportunities http://www.DoDbusopps.com

DoD Defense Standardization Program http://www.dsp.dla.mil

DON Research, Development and Acquisition http://acquisition.navy.mil/rda

Dictionary of Military & Associated Term s http://www.dtic.mil/doctrine/jel/DoDdict/

Federal Acquisition Regulations http://www.arnet.gov/far

Federal Business Opportunities http://www.fedbizopps.gov/

Fleet Industrial Supply Center (FISC) https://www.navsup.navy.mil/navsup/ourteam/comfiscs/fiscsd

General Services Administration http://www.gsa.gov

Marine Corps Systems Command (MCSC) http://www.marcorsyscom.usmc.mil

Military Sealift Command (MSC) http://www.msc.navy.mil/N10/CONTHP.htm

National Association of Purchasing Management (NAPM) http://www.napm.org

National Contract Management Association (NCMA) http://www.ncmahq.org

Naval Supply Systems Command http://www.navsup.navy.mil

Navy Electronic Commerce Online https://www.neco.navy.mil/

North American Industrial Classification Standards (NAICS) http://www.census.gov/epcd/www/naics.html

Office of Naval Research (ONR) http://www.onr.navy.mil/02/bus_op.htm

OSD Office of Small Business Programs http://www.acq.osd.mil/osbp/doing_business/index.htm

Procurement Technical Assistance Center http://www.aptac-us.org/new/

Space & Naval Warfare (SPAWAR) https://e-commerce.spawar.navy.mil

Subcontracting Resources http://www.sba.gov/GC/sbsd.html

United States Navy http://www.navy.mil

www.ingramcontent.com/pod-product-compliance
Lightning Source LLC
Chambersburg PA
CBHW080912290526

45795CB00007BA/2506